MY ANIMAL KINGDOM

PANDAS

Brown Watson

ENGLAND

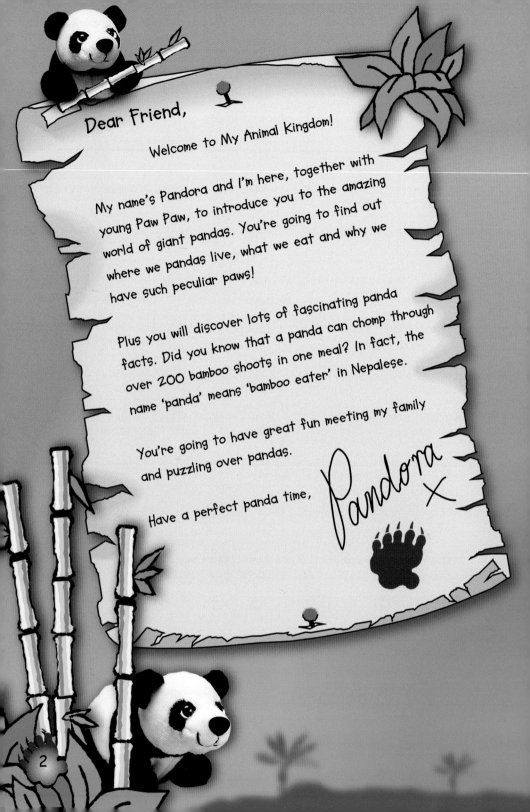

Dear Friend,

Welcome to My Animal Kingdom!

My name's Pandora and I'm here, together with young Paw Paw, to introduce you to the amazing world of giant pandas. You're going to find out where we pandas live, what we eat and why we have such peculiar paws!

Plus you will discover lots of fascinating panda facts. Did you know that a panda can chomp through over 200 bamboo shoots in one meal? In fact, the name 'panda' means 'bamboo eater' in Nepalese.

You're going to have great fun meeting my family and puzzling over pandas.

Have a perfect panda time,

Pandora x

CONTENTS

Follow us to find out more!

3

Giant pandas are big animals but they are not really giants. They are called giant pandas because they are so much bigger than their smaller cousins, the red pandas. Even though giant pandas have a striking black and white coat, they are difficult to spot because they are very shy. They are also very rare. Experts believe there are fewer than one thousand pandas left in the world.

My thick, oily fur helps keep me warm and dry in snowy weather.

I waddle along with my toes pointing in towards each other.

I have strong legs.

DID YOU KNOW?

CAT-LIKE?

● The giant panda's scientific name, *Ailuropoda melanoleuca*, means black and white cat-foot.

● The Chinese name for the giant panda is 'daxiong mao', which means great bear-cat.

● Pandas do have cat-like paws and, like cats, they can see in the dark and can climb trees. But otherwise pandas aren't really like cats at all!

My black and white coat helps me hide in the shadows in snowy forests.

I have sharp hearing so I can easily sense danger.

My eyes are just like cats' eyes. They let in extra light so that I can see well in the dark.

I have an extra-sensitive nose to sniff out the smells left by other pandas.

My teeth need to be very strong for munching through bamboo.

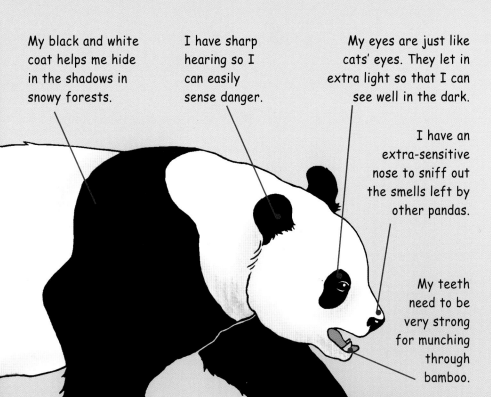

PANDA FACTS

LATIN NAME: Ailuropoda melanoleuca

ANIMAL GROUP: mammal

ANIMAL FAMILY: Ailuropods

COLOUR: black and white

SIZE: 1.2–1.5 m long. Males can measure up to 1 m from foot to shoulder, while females are usually a bit smaller.

WEIGHT: 85–120 kg

SPEED: pandas walk very slowly and rarely even break into a jog!

EATS: bamboo shoots, stalks and leaves, flowers and small animals

DRINKS: lots of water – pandas make sure they are never far from a good supply of water

LIVES: up to 25 years

5

Giant pandas have two special pieces of equipment to help them survive: their teeth and their toes! In the wild, the giant panda eats more bamboo than anything else. Bamboo is a very tough plant, so, over thousands of years, pandas have developed big, strong teeth. Their molar teeth are very wide and flat – perfect for crushing hard stalks. A strong man can't break a thick piece of fresh bamboo in half using both hands, but a panda can snap it in two with one bite! A panda's sharp claws also help it to tear off and hold bamboo shoots. Pandas use their teeth and claws to defend themselves too.

I love to crunch bamboo

PAWS FOR THOUGHT!

Sharp claws for tearing, gripping and climbing

Big pads protect the panda's foot

False thumb for extra grip

Pandas have special paws to help them hold bamboo and other plants – they have a thumb on each front paw. It's not like the thumb you have. It's actually a long wrist bone. But pandas use their false thumb in the same way as you use your thumb – to get a good grip on delicate and tough things.

CLIMBING BEARS

Pandas love to climb trees. With their special paws and long claws, they can climb up high to escape from danger or any unwanted visitors. Going up may be easy but climbing down can be more tricky, so pandas often drop the last few metres and land with a thump!

7

MY COUNTRY

Giant pandas are an endangered species, which means that their numbers are falling and there is a risk that they will die out altogether. Although you can see giant pandas in zoos throughout the world, there is only one country where they still live in the wild and that is China. Pandas live in bamboo forests in the mountains. These forests are cold, wet and, in the winter, snowy. Bamboo forests are very dense, with lots of trees and plants – plenty of panda hiding places!

MONGOLIA

CHINA

SICHUAN PROVINCE

WOLONG RESERVE

WHERE IN THE WORLD?

Giant pandas can be found in the bamboo forests of southwestern China. They live in mountain ranges in the Sichuan and neighbouring provinces. In the wild, pandas live high in the mountains, away from people. They are usually found at an altitude of between 1,100 and 3,300 m. However, if bamboo grows higher up a mountain, pandas will climb up to reach it – they have been seen at 4,000 m.

DID YOU KNOW?

• Adult pandas spend most of their time alone.

• Each panda has a range, or territory, of 4–10 square kilometres. Although this area may overlap with another panda's territory, they try to avoid meeting each other.

• The Chinese people used to call the giant panda the hermit of the forest because pandas lived on their own and were rarely seen.

HIDE AND SEEK

During cold, snowy months, pandas are particularly well camouflaged. Their patchy coats blend into the background perfectly.

Giant pandas are shy animals who prefer to live alone. To avoid meeting other pandas, each panda marks its territory with a scent. The panda rubs its bottom against trees and rocks, leaving behind a sticky, smelly liquid. This tells other pandas to go away or run the risk of meeting another panda! The smell even tells them whether the other panda is male or female!

GOLDEN PHEASANT

This beautiful bird shares the bamboo forests with the pandas. The male golden pheasant has fantastic colouring to show off to the plainer female!

SNUB-NOSED MONKEY

A panda sitting up a tree may be joined by the unusual golden snub-nosed monkey.

FOREST FRIEND

Another neighbour that the giant panda might meet in the forest is the little pika. This animal is smaller than a rabbit and, unlike the pandas, is sociable and usually lives in family groups. However, like pandas, it's not very good at running, which is why pikas move in little jumps.

FISHING CAT

This clever cat lives near water. It is a good swimmer and a fantastic fisher, scooping up fish with its paws!

BAMBOO EATERS

RED PANDAS

These cousins of the giant panda have a varied diet, but they too like bamboo.

BAMBOO RATS

Like giant pandas, bamboo rats have large teeth to help them chew bamboo.

TAKINS

These ox-like animals are about the same size as pandas and like a bamboo treat as well.

Pandas do not live in groups. Each panda, once it has left its mother, lives on its own. However, for a few days each spring, it is the breeding season and male and female pandas need to meet up to mate. They use their sensitive noses and a variety of barks and whining sounds to find each other. At this time of year, pandas can be very noisy animals. At other times, they are very quiet. When giant pandas meet by chance in the wild, they may fight to decide whose patch they are on.

This is Paw Paw's dad, Pau Pau, having a snooze!

Me and Paw Paw having a cuddle! Soon he'll have to look after himself.

This is little Paw Paw – what a cutie pie!

Patrick's the most acrobatic panda I know. He's the tree climbing champ!

13

Baby pandas are called cubs.

When a panda cub is born, it is very, very small and vulnerable. A panda mother chooses a safe spot, like a hollow tree or cave, to give birth to her baby. To begin with, she never leaves her cub alone. But soon she has to go out to look for food – and baby comes too! A panda mum carries her baby by holding it gently in her mouth. At other times, she cradles it in her huge paws. When the cub cries for attention, the mother panda immediately soothes her baby to keep it quiet. Noise might attract dangerous panda enemies like leopards or people.

LAZING AROUND

Like all baby animals, panda cubs have a lot to learn. It takes several months before a panda cub can eat bamboo, so, while Mum is eating, there's time for her cub to play – and learn. There are always trees to climb and, if that's not appealing, Mum's back makes a good climbing frame too!

I was born in May!

BABY FILE

BIRTH

Giant pandas usually give birth to one baby. Newborn pandas are about 12 cm long, weigh around 150 g and don't have much hair. The mother feeds her baby with her milk and looks after it very carefully. Soon the cub's fur begins to appear, then its eyes open and before long it is crawling around.

SIX MONTHS TO A YEAR OLD

At about six months old, the baby begins to eat bamboo. By the time it is one year old, it no longer needs its mother's help and can look after itself.

ONE AND A HALF YEARS AND OVER

By the age of one and a half, pandas will have left their mothers. Pandas reach full maturity between the ages of four and seven years old.

15

Giant pandas need to spend up to 14 hours a day eating. Lots of people know a panda's favourite food is bamboo, but not many people realize that the ancestors of the giant panda were carnivorous – eating only meat. Over time, the panda's diet has changed and now it eats mainly plants although it cannot digest them very well. It has to eat a lot of bamboo to get enough nutrients to keep it healthy.

MUNCHING MACHINE

Pandas normally eat sitting down and preferably surrounded by bamboo! The panda reaches out and bites off a bamboo stalk. Next, it strips the tough outside from the bamboo, then it quickly munches the stalk. Yummy!

BEST BAMBOO

Bamboo is a type of plant. There are about 1,200 different kinds of bamboo in the world, but pandas are thought to eat only about 20 of them! Two of the wild giant pandas' favourite kinds of bamboo are called the 'cold arrow' and the 'walking stick'.

SIDE ORDERS

Up to 99 per cent of a panda's diet may be bamboo, but it does eat other things as well. Pandas are really omnivores, which means they eat both meat and plants. Small animals, such as rats, are sometimes on the menu, as are other types of plant, such as crocuses and irises.

It's all here in black and white!

DID YOU KNOW?

EAT AND SLEEP

Pandas do not sleep at night like you do. Instead, they sleep whenever they feel like it. They wander around their territory day and night finding food and stopping to sleep where and when they want – for a few hours or just a few minutes!

NO FRIEND OF MINE!

Adult giant pandas have no natural enemies in the animal kingdom, although young pandas are at risk from some predators. The main problem for pandas is that their habitat is threatened. People are cutting back the forest to use the wood and to make way for more houses and farms. This doesn't leave a lot of room for the pandas who don't have enough space to roam freely and who can't find enough food.

FLOWERING FAMINE

Every 50-100 years, an entire species of bamboo will flower, drop its seeds and die. The seeds grow but the new bamboo does not mature for another six or seven years. When this happens, animals such as pandas lose an important food supply and may die.

POACHING PROBLEM

In China, hunting giant pandas is a capital offence, which means that the hunter can be punished by death. However, pandas are still in danger. Young pandas are caught to be put in zoos and adult pandas are still poached for their fur coats, called pelts. A single pelt can sell for US$100,000 on the black market and, for this amount of money, people are still prepared to hunt pandas illegally.

ou're safe with me!

DANGER SPOTS

Newborn panda cubs are small and vulnerable. Predators like the snow leopard will make a quick meal from a panda cub left on its own. The snow leopard, also called an ounce, is another rare, endangered animal that lives high in the mountains of Asia. Snow leopards have beautiful pearly-grey coats with black spots.

A DAY IN MY LIFE

6:00 AM Sun-up. Actually giant pandas are mostly nocturnal, so we'd been up all night. But other animals wake up now – birds are especially noisy at this time of day.

8:00 AM I like it when the sun comes up because it gets a bit warmer. I set off in search of a morning feast.

10:00 AM I found a great patch of my favourite bamboo – it looks just like lots of walking sticks. Paw Paw will be able to eat bamboo soon, so I gave him a lesson in how to find the tastiest shoots.

12 NOON We are more active at night – we can't see very much in the daytime anyway as we have special eyes for seeing in the dark. So the two of us sat down, camouflaged in the bamboo, and had a few hours sleep.

3:00 PM I woke up extremely thirsty. Luckily, we were quite close to the stream and so we didn't have to go far to find a nice long drink of water.

5:00 PM A few more hours sleep to work up a good appetite for the night ahead!

7:00 PM Night time but I was wide awake! Thought I heard a leopard and we climbed up a tree to try and hide. It went away, though, so we soon came down again.

9:00 PM

we heard some very loud rushing and, just as we hid behind a few trees, we saw some people. We often see people. They never seem to want to harm us but I'd rather not find out. You never know.

12 MIDNIGHT

We slipped into another panda's home range by mistake. It belonged to Pau Pau, Paw Paw's father, but I didn't want to see him. Luckily, he'd left his scent mark on some trees to warn us he was around, so we managed to avoid him.

2.00 AM

I found some flowers to eat – they were yummy, but not quite as tasty as bamboo! Paw Paw was practising crawling – he had a shock when he fell off my shoulder.

4.30 AM

There were rats in my bamboo! If I'd been able to catch one, it would have made a nice dinner treat. I'm not a brilliant hunter, so the rats escaped. Never mind, better luck next time!

5.30 AM

I began to feel tired. Still, I wasn't quite full and didn't see why I should stop eating when I was surrounded by food!

Pandora x

BEARS AND ME

Ever since giant pandas were first seen by people in Europe, zoologists (scientists who study animals) have been unable to decide whether pandas belong to the bear family or the raccoon family. Most people now think they are more like bears than raccoons.

BIG BROTHER

Giant pandas certainly look more like bears than like raccoons. The brown bear is the most common kind of bear. Like giant pandas, brown bears live alone except during the breeding season. This bear is also an omnivore and eats plants and meat.

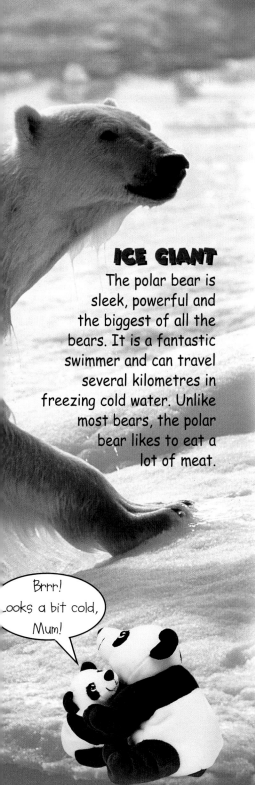

BEAR TO BEAR

The polar bear is the largest bear and can grow to over 3 m long.

Kodiak bears are similar to grizzly bears, only a bit bigger!

Grizzlies are perhaps the most aggressive of the bears.

Giant pandas are only half the size of polar bears.

ICE GIANT

The polar bear is sleek, powerful and the biggest of all the bears. It is a fantastic swimmer and can travel several kilometres in freezing cold water. Unlike most bears, the polar bear likes to eat a lot of meat.

Brrr! Looks a bit cold, Mum!

BIG BEARS

The blood of giant pandas is very similar to bears' blood, and giant pandas have the same heavy body shape and short tails as bears. Some of the giant panda's bear cousins are real giants, though, and make pandas look small!

The giant panda's closest relative is the red, or lesser, panda. Giant pandas are now thought to be more closely related to bears, but red pandas are definitely like raccoons. Giant and red pandas may look different but they share several characteristics. Like giant pandas, red pandas eat a lot of bamboo and have a special 'false thumb'. Both types of panda also have similar skull, foot and tooth structures, which sets them apart from other bears and raccoons.

RED PANDAS

The red panda is mainly a nocturnal animal, spending its days curled up on a branch with its beautiful long, bushy tail covering its head, or with its head tucked into its chest. At night time, it comes out to forage for food – looking for bamboo shoots, other roots and fruit, and even small animals.

PLEISTOCENE PANDAS!

Giant pandas have been around for thousands of years. In fact, their ancestors can be traced back to the Pleistocene Age, around 2 million years ago! Giant pandas may now only live in China but they used to be much more widespread. Many years ago, pandas lived in other Asian countries, such as Burma and Vietnam, as well as throughout China. Sadly, changes in the climate and the growth of towns and cities have pushed pandas back into a very limited area now.

Aren't we an interesting family!

RING-TAILED RACCOON

Raccoons are easy to recognize by their long, ringed tails and the mask-like band across their faces. People in North America call raccoons 'coons', for short. Some Americans even have pet raccoons. Raccoons are happy on the ground, up trees or even in the water!

Giant pandas were a well-kept Chinese secret until the late 1860s, when a French missionary priest, Père David, sent back the first panda pelt and skeleton to Europe from China. But it was not until the 1930s that western eyes saw living pandas for the first time. The Chinese knew how special the giant panda was. For hundreds of years, they believed it was rather like a god. Although people are part of the reason why pandas are under such threat, many organisations are now trying to help save the giant panda.

PANDAS IN RESERVE

Giant pandas are an endangered species. In China, there are special reserves for pandas, such as the Wolong Reserve. Here, pandas can live in safety. The WWF (World Wildlife Fund) which helps to protect rare animals, has a giant panda as its famous logo.

BEHIND BARS

Pandas are rare and any zoo that has one is very lucky. Lots of people like to come and see pandas but not many zoos have one. The dealer who bought the famous Chi-Chi for London Zoo from China had to swap her for three giraffes, two rhinos, two hippos and two zebra!

My Dad knew Chi–Chi!

WHAT DOES IT MEAN?

ALTITUDE

This is the height of something – usually how high something is above the level of the sea.

BLACK MARKET

It is called a black market when people buy and sell things which the law forbids or restricts the sale of - such as rare animals.

HERMIT

A hermit is a person who lives alone and hides away from everyone else.

MOLAR

Molars are the flat, wide teeth at the back of the mouth. They are used for grinding up hard, crunchy food like bamboo.

NOCTURNAL

A nocturnal animal is an animal that sleeps during the day and is active at night.